MISSION SIXPACK

BY MIGHTY MIND WARRIOR

Publisher: BoD · Books on Demand GmbH,
In de Tarpen 42, 22848 Norderstedt, bod@bod.de
Print: Libri Plureos GmbH, Friedensallee 273,
22763 Hamburg

For questions and suggestions:

www.mightymindwarrior.ch

1st edition 2025
ISBN: 978-3-7583-3960-8

For more information visit
www.mightymindwarrior.ch

www.instagram.com/mightymindwarrior

TABLE OF CONTENTS

1.
INTRODUCTION

Are you ready to unveil those stunning six-pack abs? Achieving this goal requires more than just targeted ab workouts; it demands a holistic approach that combines core strengthening with overall body fat reduction. Dive into our exhilarating 30-day plan, featuring just 15 minutes of intense bodyweight training each day! This program is expertly crafted to empower you to sculpt and tone your core while accelerating your journey to a leaner physique. Let's ignite your transformation and unlock your full potential!

GOOD LUCK WITH YOUR WORKOUT!

2.

WARM-UP, COOL-DOWN

WARM-UP

Your Key to Unlocking Peak Performance!

NO EXCUSES
WARMING UP IS NON-NEGOTIABLE!

To unlock your full potential and safeguard against injuries, dedicating just 2-5 minutes to a dynamic warm-up before every workout is crucial. Here's why you should always prioritize warming up:

1. **Prepare Your Body for Greatness:**
   A solid warm-up activates your entire body, setting the stage for optimal performance in every movement you make.

2. **Energize Your Muscles:**
   By increasing blood flow and enhancing flexibility, a warm-

up equips your muscles with the readiness they need to tackle any challenge and helps prevent injuries.

3. **Injury Prevention is Key:**
   A comprehensive warm-up significantly reduces the risk of strains and joint overload, keeping you in the game and on track.

4. **Boost Performance and Speed Up Recovery:**
   Get ready to unleash your power! Warming up not only enhances your strength but also aids in faster recovery, making your training sessions more effective.

5. **Elevate Your Heart Rate:**
   Gradually increasing your heart rate gently primes your cardiovascular system for the intensity ahead.

6. **Enhance Flexibility for Better Execution:**
   Warming up effectively boosts flexibility, allowing you to perform exercises safely and with greater precision.

In essence, an effective warm-up primes both your body and mind for the workout ahead, amplifying your efficiency and propelling you toward your long-term fitness goals. This is especially vital for plyometric exercises as they demand agility and quick response!

Remember: invest in your warm-up, and reap the rewards in every session!

Enhanced Warm-Up Options

Prepare your body for action with these dynamic warm-up exercises that will get your heart pumping and your muscles activated:

1. **Leg Raises:**
   Alternately lift your legs to energize your leg muscles and hip flexors, setting the stage for a powerful workout.

2. **Light Jogging:**
   Hit the ground running at a comfortable pace to boost circulation and warm up those leg muscles effectively.

3. **Jogging in Place:**
   No room to run? No problem! Jogging on the spot is a fantastic way to elevate your heart rate and warm up wherever you are.

4. **Light Squats:**
   Ease into your workout with gentle squats that engage your thighs and prepare them for more intense movements.

5. **Jump Rope:**
   Elevate your heart rate dynamically! Skipping rope works your whole body while giving your cardiovascular system a solid boost.

6. **Dynamic Leg Extensions:**
   Engage those thigh and hip muscles with powerful leg movements designed to enhance flexibility and strength.

7. **Dynamic Arm Stretches:**
   Activate your shoulders and arms by dynamically reaching, allowing for a smoother workout ahead.

8. **Arm Circles:**
   Mobilize your shoulder muscles by performing arm circles, preparing them for the challenges ahead.

9. **Jumping Jacks:**
   Get your blood flowing with this classic exercise that stimulates the cardiovascular system while activating major muscle groups.

10. **Lunges:**
    Step forward into lunges to engage your legs and glutes, preparing your body for movement-focused training.

11. **Light Cardio Exercises:**
Incorporate simple activities like brisk walking or gentle hops to elevate your heart rate without overexertion.

12. **Dynamic Stretching:**
Infuse movement into stretching to improve flexibility and ready your muscles for the workout ahead.

13. **Gentle Rotational Movements:**
Loosen up with gentle upper body rotations, promoting spine mobility and core engagement.

14. **Easy Running:**
A moderate-paced run helps transition your body slowly into more vigorous activity.

15. **Hip Circles:**
Enhance hip mobility and flexibility by performing circular motions with your hips.

16. **Gentle Loosening Exercises:**
Use simple movements to prepare every part of your body for the main event.

17. **Leg Swings:**
Swinging your legs forward and backward warms up lower extremity muscles and joints effectively.

18. **Shoulder Circles:**
Release tension in your shoulders with shoulder circles, ensuring they're ready for action.

19. **Body Rotations:**
Rotate gently from side to side to engage and mobilize your core muscles thoroughly.

20. **Light Planks:**
Activate and stabilize your core with a modified plank, preparing it for more demanding exercises.

21.**Walking in Place:**
   Move freely in limited space by walking in place, warming up the entire body effortlessly.

Get started with these energizing warm-up options to enhance not just flexibility but also overall performance! It's time to unleash your potential and conquer any workout with confidence!

THE ESSENTIAL CONCLUSION TO YOUR TRAINING SESSION

Every training session should always conclude with a well-structured cool-down phase lasting a few minutes. This crucial period serves multiple purposes:

- **Promotes Muscle Stretching:**
  Helps in elongating the muscles, enhancing flexibility.

- **Stabilizes Heart Rate:**
  Aids in gradually bringing your heart rate back to its resting state.

- **Reduces Risk of Injury:**
  Softens the impact on your body, minimizing potential injuries.

- **Optimizes Recovery:**
  Supports the body in bouncing back more efficiently post-exercise.

- **Enhances Training Effectiveness:**
  Solidifies the gains made during your workout.

- **Stretches and Relaxes Trained Muscles:**
  Eases tension in the muscles that have been engaged.

- **Prepares Muscles for Future Strain:**
  Gets your muscles ready for the next challenge.

- **Improves Flexibility:**
  Increases overall range of motion.

- **Shortens Recovery Time:**
  Facilitates quicker recovery between sessions.

For an effective cool-down phase, consider incorporating the following activities:

1. **Stretching:**
   This fundamental practice increases muscle flexibility and boosts blood circulation.

2. **Targeted Stretching Exercises:**
   Engage in specific stretches that alleviate tension and enhance mobility.

3. **Light Jogging:**
   A gradual jog or easy run helps lower your heart rate methodically while further promoting circulation.

4. **Walking:**
   A moderate-paced walk can aid in normalizing your heart rate and relaxing your muscles at the same time.

5. **Yoga or Pilates:**
   Gentle sessions of yoga or Pilates not only support muscle relaxation but also enhance flexibility.

6. **Foam Rolling (Fascial Training):**
   Utilizing a foam roller releases muscle tension and massages sore areas effectively.

7. **Breathing Exercises:**
   Focused breathing calms the nervous system, helping you unwind post-training.

8. **Gentle Gymnastics Movements:**
   Incorporate light movements like arm circles or gentle hip bends to gradually ease your body down.

Incorporating these cool-down strategies into your routine will leave you feeling rejuvenated and prepared for your next workout!

UNLOCK YOUR FULL POTENTIAL

After those intense workouts, allowing adequate time for recovery is essential to maximize your performance and prepare for the challenges ahead. Tailor your rest periods to your current fitness level, ensuring you're set up for success in the week to come.

Remember, a rest day doesn't mean "doing nothing." While complete inactivity is an option, embracing active recovery through light activities can yield far greater benefits. On these days, steer clear of high-intensity exercises. Instead, indulge in gentle movements that promote relaxation, enhance blood flow, and support your recovery journey.

Here are some invigorating activities you can include in your recovery routine:

- **Breathing Exercises:**
  Center your mind and body.

- **Light Mobility Routines:**
  Engage in mobility exercises to maintain flexibility.

- **Light Cardio Training:**
  Enjoy a leisurely run or easy cycling session.

- **Stretching Exercises:**
  Embrace gentle stretches to alleviate tension.

- **Yoga or Pilates:**
  Discover tranquility through subtle movement.

- **Nature Walks:**
  Breathe in fresh air on a calming stroll.

- **Qigong:**
  Experience the harmony of movement and energy.

- **Mindfulness Training:**
  Cultivate mental resilience through focused awareness.

- **Gentle Movement Meditation:**
  Enhance body awareness through gentle flow.

- **Tactical Movements:**
  Incorporate rolling or crawling for playful engagement.

- **Swimming:**
  Soothe your muscles with the buoyancy of water.

- **Hiking:**
  Combine nature and movement for rejuvenation.

- **Deep Relaxation Techniques:**
  Surrender to restorative practices.

HYDRATION & NUTRITION

FUEL YOUR RECOVERY

To truly reap the rewards of your hard work, prioritize hydration, nutrition, and sleep. Staying well-hydrated and consuming a balanced diet are vital components for optimizing performance and enhancing recovery. The synergy of proper fluid intake, nutritious meals, and restful slumber not only boosts your physical capabilities but also fortifies your ability to tackle physical challenges head-on.

Ensure you give your muscles the opportunity to recover deeply and grow stronger by adhering to these fundamental principles:

- Drink plenty of water every day.

- Maintain a balanced diet rich in nutrients.

- Prioritize quality sleep above all.

BREATHE YOUR WAY TO PEAK PERFORMANCE

A Comprehensive Guide to Optimal Oxygenation and Endurance

The Power of Breath:
Breathing is not just a natural process; it's the cornerstone of your endurance and overall performance. Deep, even breaths are essential for delivering the oxygen your body craves during exercise. When you prioritize controlled breathing, you enhance oxygen flow and sharpen muscle control. Don't underestimate the impact of your breath—it's your secret weapon in conquering physical challenges!

Mastering Basic Breathing Techniques:
To fuel your muscles and boost endurance, adopt a deep and steady breathing pattern.

- **Rhythmic Breathing Cycle:**
  Inhale through your nose and exhale through your mouth in a steady rhythm.

- **Consistency is Key:**
  Maintain this breathing rhythm throughout your workout to maximize oxygenation.

Tailoring Your Breath to Different Training Phases:

- **Stretching Exercises:**
  Engage in deep, even breathing to relax your body and deliver vital oxygen to your muscles.

- **Strength Training:**
  Inhale as you lift and exhale as you lower—inhale while extending your limbs and exhale when returning to the starting position.

- **High-Intensity Workouts:**
  Keep your breath deep and steady, even during intense moments. Inhale before you jump and exhale upon landing.

Synchronizing Breath with Movement:

- **Movement-Dependent Breathing:**
  Coordinate your breath with each motion—inhale as you lower yourself and exhale as you push up. This synchronization optimizes blood flow and elevates oxygen delivery to working muscles.

- **Lateral Movements:**
  Inhale as you return to center and exhale when moving sideways for a balanced approach.

Cultivating Consistency Under Pressure:
Even when the going gets tough, maintaining controlled and rhythmic breathing is crucial for maximizing oxygen intake. Your breath can be the lifeline that keeps you focused and

strong under exertion.

Practical Breathing Technique Exercises:

1. **Establish a Steady Rhythm:**
    Focus on avoiding irregular breaths; consistency
    enhances overall performance.

2. **Sync Breathing with Movement:**
    Aligning your breath with your actions amplifies
    exercise efficiency and recruits muscles more
    effectively.

By integrating these breathing techniques, you won't just
elevate your physical capabilities—you'll also fortify your
mental resilience and endurance. Breathe deeply, move
powerfully, and unleash your full potential!

3.
WEEK 1
BUILDING THE BASICS

Day 1:
Full Body Foundations

- **Warm-Up:**
  3 minutes of Jumping Jacks to get the heart rate up.

- **Core Strength**:

  - 2 sets of 30 seconds Planks

  - 2 sets of 30 seconds Side Planks (each side)

- **Dynamic Movement**:
  2 sets of 15 Russian Twists (each side)

- **Slow-Motion Stability**:
  1 set of 10 Slow-Motion Mountain Climbers (focus on core stability)

- **Core Crunch**:
  2 sets of 15 Crunches

Day 2:
Legs and Core Power

- **Warm-Up:**
  3 minutes of Burpees to energize the body.

- **Leg Strength:**

  - 3 sets of 30 seconds Wall Sit

  - 2 sets of 20 Lunges (each leg)

- **Core Stabilization:**
  2 sets of 20 seconds Hollow Hold

- **Cycling Abs:**
  2 sets of 15 Bicycle Crunches (each side)

Day 3:
Cardio & Core Blast

- **Warm-Up:**
  Get your heart racing with 3 minutes of High Knees.

- **Sprinting:**
  2 sets of 30 seconds Sprinting in Place

- **Core Builders:**

  - 3 sets of 30 seconds Leg Raises

  - 2 sets of 15 V-Ups

- **Ab Rollouts:**
  2 sets of 15 Abs Rollouts (with or without an ab wheel)

Day 4:
Core Stabilization Techniques

- **Warm-Up:**
  Mimic rope skipping for 3 minutes.

- **Plank Hold:**

  - 3 sets of 40 seconds Plank

  - 3 sets of 30 seconds Superman Hold

- **Side Strength:**
  2 sets of 30 seconds Side Plank (each side)

Day 5:
Upper Body & Core Integration

- **Warm-Up:**
  Build momentum with arm circles for 3 minutes.

- **Upper Body Strength:**

  - 3 sets of 15 Push-Ups

  - 2 sets of 30 seconds Plank Shoulder Taps

- **Challenge Yourself with:**
  2 sets of 15 Spiderman Push-Ups

Day 6:
Dynamic Core Engagement

- **Warm-Up:**
  Get active with jumping for 3 minutes.

- **Power Moves:**
  3 sets of 10 Jump Squats

- **Cardio Burst:**
  3 sets of 20 seconds Mountain Climbers

- **Oblique Focus:**
  2 sets of 15 Oblique V-Ups (each side)

- **Rotational Strength:**
  2 sets of 30 seconds Russian Twists

Day 7:
Active Recovery – Stretch It Out

- Spend a rejuvenating **15 minutes on full-body stretching**, allowing your muscles to recover and recharge for the week ahead.

Stay strong and committed as you lay the groundwork this week! Let's push boundaries together and unlock your full potential!

4.
WEEK 2 - 4
ELEVATE YOUR INTENSITY

As you step into Week 2, it's time to ramp up your workout intensity! Let's challenge those limits by increasing the number of sets or repetitions and minimizing rest times between exercises.

Repetition & Set Adjustments:

- **Planks and Side Planks:** Add an additional 10 seconds each week to strengthen your core further.

- **Dynamic Exercises:** Aim for 5 more reps per set each week to amplify your endurance and power.

- **Superman Holds:** Increase your hold time by 5 seconds weekly, or add an extra set to enhance your back strength.

- **Cardio Elements:** Boost your cardio by adding an extra minute each week to elevate your heart rate and stamina.

Remember, Day 7 is a well-deserved rest day, dedicated to stretching exercises to promote recovery and flexibility. Let's stay focused, determined, and ready to achieve your full potential! Keep pushing the boundaries and celebrate every step of this journey!

5.
COMPREHENSIVE GUIDE

AB ROLLOUTS

Introduction to Ab Rollouts

Ab rollouts are a potent exercise designed to engage and strengthen your core muscles while also targeting your shoulders, arms, and lower back. This move emphasizes control and stability, making it a versatile addition to your fitness routine. You can perform ab rollouts using various equipment such as an ab roller, dumbbells, or even an exercise ball.

Benefits of Ab Rollouts

Primarily focusing on your core, including the abdominals and lower back, ab rollouts also engage shoulder muscles, promoting stability throughout the body. The controlled motion challenges not just the core but also the body's stabilizers for a comprehensive workout.

Steps for Performing Ab Rollouts

1. **Starting Position:**
   Kneel on a mat and grasp the ab roller with both hands, extending your arms in front of you. Ensure your shoulders are positioned directly above the ab roller and that your knees are hip-width apart.

2. **Core Stabilization:**
Activate your core by tightening your abdominal muscles while keeping your spine in a neutral alignment. Avoid slumping or hyperextending your lower back to maintain proper form.

3. **The Rollout:**
Begin rolling the ab roller forward slowly and with control, keeping your arms straight. Progress only as far as you can without losing control over your core muscles; aim for minimal hip drop, with most of the motion originating from your shoulders and arms.

4. **Return to Starting Position:**
Pull the ab roller back towards you gradually, re-engaging your core and lifting your hips minimally. Keep your abdominal muscles contracted to protect your lower back throughout this movement.

Common Mistakes & Corrections

- **Back Sagging:**
To prevent sagging in the lower back, remain vigilant about keeping your core engaged during the rollout.

- **Uncontrolled Movements:**
Always perform the rollout slowly; this maximizes muscle engagement while minimizing injury risks.

- **Rolling Too Far:**
Limit how far you roll forward to ensure that you can maintain control of your core, thus avoiding potential strain or injury.

Variations to Elevate Your Routine:

- **Dumbbell Ab Rollouts:**
Substitute an ab roller with two dumbbells placed

parallel on the floor. Roll them forward simultaneously for a challenging twist.

- **Exercise Ball Ab Rollouts:**
  Place your forearms on an exercise ball while maintaining a plank position. Control the movement as you roll the ball forward and return.

- **Standing Ab Rollouts:**
  Begin standing with bent knees and the ab roller on the floor ahead of you. Gradually roll it forward until almost parallel to the ground before returning.

- **Single-Arm Ab Rollouts:**
  Challenge yourself by using just one hand on the ab roller while resting the opposite hand on your hip. Alternate sides after each rep or set for balanced muscle engagement.

- **Ab Rollouts from Your Feet:**
  For seasoned athletes, try performing rollouts from a plank position (on your feet) instead of your knees, demanding greater core strength and intensity.

Alternative Exercises

If traditional ab rollouts pose joint issues, consider these alternatives to achieve similar benefits:

- **Plank Walkouts:**
  Start standing, bend forward, and walk hands out into a plank before walking them back up. This strengthens both core and shoulder muscles.

- **Stability Ball Pike:**
  While in a plank position on an exercise ball, slowly roll it towards your chest until hips rise—then return to plank form.

- **Hollow Body Hold:**
  Lie on your back with legs and shoulders slightly elevated off the ground; hold this position to activate and strengthen abdominal muscles.

Conclusion

Ab rollouts stand out as an effective exercise for fortifying core muscles, shoulders, and arms. By mastering technique and exploring various adaptations, you can tailor this exercise to match your fitness level. Embrace ab rollouts as part of your regimen to unlock their myriad benefits and enhance overall physical performance!

THE ULTIMATE FULL-BODY WORKOUT

Burpees are a powerhouse of an exercise, expertly designed to build strength and endurance while elevating your heart rate. They are a staple in high-intensity interval training (HIIT) due to their dynamic nature, combining multiple movements into one fluid sequence. Despite their challenging reputation, burpees are an incredibly effective way to enhance cardiovascular fitness and push your physical limits.

How to Execute a Burpee with Precision:

1. **Starting Position:**
   Stand tall with your feet shoulder-width apart and arms relaxed at your sides. Embrace the challenge ahead!

2. **Squat Down:**
   Engage your core as you bend your knees and lower into a squat, reaching your arms forward to maintain balance.

3. **Hands on the Floor:**
   Place your hands firmly on the ground just in front of your feet, about shoulder-width apart. Feel the shift in energy as you prepare for the next move!

4. **Jump Back:**
   Propel yourself backward with both feet, landing in a strong push-up position (plank). Your body should form a straight line from head to heels—this is where strength meets stability.

5. **Push-Up (Optional):**
   For added intensity, lower yourself into a push-up at this stage. This extra challenge will build upper body strength and resilience.

6. **Jump Forward:**
   From the push-up position, spring your feet back toward your hands. Picture every jump as a step closer to your goals!

7. **Return to Standing Position:**
   Rise from the squat, grounding yourself once more in an upright stance, ready for action.

8. **Final Jump:**
   Launch into an explosive jump from this standing position, reaching for the sky as you clap your hands above your head—celebrate the movement you've just conquered!

Incorporating Burpees into Your Workout Routine: Challenge yourself with multiple burpees in succession or integrate them into an interval training session for maximum impact. Each burpee serves as an opportunity to strengthen not just your body but also your mental resilience as you master this full-body movement.

Embrace the burn and feel empowered as you elevate your fitness journey!

BICYCLE CRUNCHES

YOUR PATH TO STRONGER OBLIQUES AND CORE

Bicycle crunches are a dynamic and highly effective exercise that targets not only your obliques but also the rectus abdominis (commonly known as the "six-pack muscle") and deeper abdominal muscles. This engaging movement mimics the action of pedaling a bicycle while incorporating essential rotations of the upper body, delivering a comprehensive workout for your core.

How to Perform Bicycle Crunches Correctly:

1. **Starting Position:**
   Begin by lying on your back with your feet flat on the floor and your knees bent. Position your hands gently beside your head or behind your ears, keeping your fingers relaxed and unlinked.

2. **Upper Body Lift:**
   Elevate your upper body slightly off the ground to engage your abdominal muscles. Remember to keep your neck relaxed to prevent strain during this movement.

3. **Initiate Leg Movement:**
   Draw your right knee toward your chest while extending your left leg. Ensure your left leg remains just above the floor, creating tension in your core.

4. **Upper Body Rotation:**
   Twist your upper body, guiding your left elbow toward your right knee as you draw it in. Avoid touching the elbow to the knee; instead, focus on the rotational movement that engages the obliques.

5. **Switching Positions:**
   Seamlessly transition by pulling in your left knee and extending your right leg, while rotating your upper body to bring your right elbow toward the left knee. Imagine you're cycling through this movement!

6. **Continue the Rhythm:**
   Keep alternating these movements at a steady, controlled pace. Your legs should maintain a smooth motion, and ensure each elbow approaches its opposite knee as you cycle through.

Tips for Maximizing Bicycle Crunches:

- Focus on using your abs rather than momentum to drive each movement.

- Keep a neutral neck position by directing your gaze toward the ceiling or a spot on the wall in front of you—avoid pulling on your head.

- Maintain tight abdominal contraction throughout the duration of the exercise.

- For an added challenge, slow down the motion, concentrating on each rotation and the trajectory of your elbow.

Bicycle crunches may test your limits, but they are a powerful exercise for sculpting strong and defined abs. Incorporate this versatile core workout into your routine regularly, and watch as you build resilience and strength in both body and mind! Remember, every rep counts toward achieving your fitness goals!

CRUNCHES

UNLOCKING CORE STRENGTH

C runches are a classic and widely recognized exercise for enhancing abdominal strength. Regularly incorporated into fitness routines, they form the cornerstone of developing a powerful core. While crunches may appear straightforward, executing them with the correct technique is essential for maximizing benefits and minimizing the risk of injury.

Step-by-Step Guide to Perfecting Your Crunches:

1. **Starting Position:**
   Lie flat on your back on an exercise mat. Bend your knees and place your feet firmly on the floor, approximately hip-width apart. Position your hands gently behind your head, ensuring you're not pulling on your neck, or alternatively, cross your arms over your chest.

2. **Engage Your Core:**
   Before initiating the movement, activate your abdominal muscles by drawing your belly button towards your spine. This crucial "core tension" should be maintained throughout the entire exercise for optimal effectiveness.

3. **The Crunch:**
   Exhale as you lift your upper body—your shoulders and upper spine—off the ground by contracting your abdominal muscles. Keep your lower back pressed against the floor. Raise only as high as feels comfortable while ensuring you don't strain your neck or shoulders.

4. **The Return:**
   Inhale deeply and slowly lower your upper body back to the starting position in a controlled manner. Focus on maintaining intentional movement without relying on momentum.

5. **Repetitions:**
   Aim for 2-3 sets of 10-15 repetitions, adjusting according to your fitness level and training goals.

Tips for Effective Execution:

- **Protect Your Neck:**
  Avoid pulling on your neck to prevent discomfort and ensure the focus remains on engaging those vital abdominal muscles.

- **Prioritize Controlled Movements:**
  Steer clear of jerky or rapid motions, which can compromise effectiveness and lead to injury. Maintain steady and deliberate movements throughout.

- **Keep Core Tension:**S
  ustain tension in your abdominal muscles even during the return phase to reinforce engagement and maximize strength development.

Common Mistakes to Avoid During Crunches:

- **Using Momentum:**
  Relying on momentum to propel yourself up detracts from abdominal engagement and can lead to back discomfort.

- **Overly High Elbow Position:**
  Ensure elbows are kept wide apart and out of your line of sight to properly activate the abdominal muscles.

- **Excessive Lift:**
  It's not necessary to lift your entire back off the mat; focus on effectively contracting those core muscles instead.

Crunches are a fantastic exercise for targeting the front abdominal muscles, offering versatility through modifications such as adding twists for oblique engagement. When executed properly, this effective move not only enhances core strength but also promotes better posture and increased stability—empowering you to tackle physical challenges with confidence!

ENHANCE YOUR CORE TRAINING

The hollow hold is a fundamental exercise for core training, widely utilized in gymnastics and fitness practices. This dynamic position not only strengthens your abdominal muscles but also lays a solid foundation for improved posture and powerful movement sequences. To unlock the full benefits of this exercise, it's essential to prioritize proper execution. Here's your guide to mastering the hollow hold while avoiding common pitfalls.

Step-by-Step Instructions for the Hollow Hold:

1. **Start on Your Back:**
   Lie flat on a comfortable, firm surface, such as an exercise mat. Position your arms alongside your body, legs straight, and feet together.

2. **Press Your Lower Back into the Floor:**
   Engage your abdominal muscles to actively press your lower back into the floor. This helps maintain a neutral spine and protects against injury.

3. **Raise Your Shoulders and Arms:**
   Lift your shoulder blades off the ground while extending your arms alongside your ears or above your head. Ensure that your neck remains in a neutral position by gazing between your arms or at your feet.

4. **Leg Lift:**
   Extend your legs, raising them off the floor while keeping them together. The level of difficulty increases as you lower your legs—maintain contact between your lower back and the floor for optimal effectiveness.

5. **Hold the Position:**
   Maintain tension in this position for the prescribed duration or as long as you can without sacrificing form. Remember to breathe steadily to further engage your core muscles.

6. **Controlled Release:**
   Lower your arms and legs back to the floor gracefully while allowing your muscles to relax.

Tips for Effective Execution:

- **Engage Your Core:**
  Actively engage your abdominal muscles throughout to safeguard your lower back.

- **Progress Gradually:**
  Start with higher leg positions and work down as you build strength.

- **Short Intervals:**
  Begin with brief holds (10-20 seconds) and increase duration progressively to enhance muscle endurance.

Common Mistakes to Avoid:

- **Hollow Back:**
  If your lower back lifts off the floor, you compromise the

integrity of the exercise and risk back pain. Keep consistent core engagement to avoid this issue.

- **Inadequate Leg Positioning:**
  Beginners often lower their legs too much, leading to loss of tension. Start with elevated legs until you master the technique.

- **Shoulders Raised:**
  Keep shoulders relaxed and away from the ears to minimize neck strain.

- **Neck Overextension:**
  Maintain a forward gaze to prevent unnecessary neck stress.

The hollow hold is a challenging yet highly effective exercise that stabilizes your core and supports a wide range of movements. By following these guidelines, you can perform this exercise safely while minimizing injury risk. Remember, quality and body tension are far more crucial than duration or repetitions; practice diligently and consistently to see remarkable progress in your core strength!

ELEVATE YOUR WORKOUT WARM-UP

High knees, also known as knee lifts, are an exhilarating dynamic warm-up exercise that energizes both your muscles and cardiovascular system while enhancing coordination. Commonly included in runners' training regimens, they also play a pivotal role in various fitness and sports programs. Whether performed alone or as part of a comprehensive warm-up sequence, high knees effectively raise your body temperature and prepare your legs for more intense challenges ahead.

How to Perform High Knees Correctly:

1. **Starting Position:**
   Begin by standing tall with your knees slightly bent and feet hip-width apart. Keep your gaze forward and maintain an upright posture. Extend your arms in front of you with

palms at hip height; this positioning will create a target for your lifting knees.

2. **Movement Sequence:**
   Kick off the exercise by lifting your right knee towards your right palm, aiming for a crisp touch. Bring that foot back down and quickly switch to driving your left knee up towards your left palm. Picture this movement as marching on the spot, but with an emphasis on elevating the knees high!

3. **Pace and Intensity:**
   As you gain confidence, ramp up the pace by alternating feet quickly. Remember, the intensity of high knees can be adjusted by both the speed and height of your knee lifts— elevate those knees higher and push faster for an intense cardio burst!

4. **Duration:**
   You can engage in high knees either by setting timed intervals (such as 30 seconds) or by counting repetitions per leg. Start with shorter intervals or fewer reps, gradually increasing them to boost your endurance over time.

Tips for Optimal Execution:

- Focus on actively driving your knees upward rather than relying on momentum.

- Keep your upper body stable throughout the movement; avoid leaning forward excessively.

- Land gently on the balls of your feet to safeguard your joints from impact.

Incorporating high knees into your warm-up routine not only elevates your heart rate but also enhances the coordination and flexibility of your leg muscles. They are a powerful addition that prepares you to tackle any workout with confidence. Let high knees be a staple in your fitness regimen, enriching your warm-up while propelling you toward greater overall fitness and performance!

ELEVATE YOUR WORKOUT WITH THIS ENERGIZING EXERCISE!

Jumping jacks are a dynamic and invigorating full-body exercise perfect for kickstarting your workout routine. Often incorporated as a warm-up or within high-intensity interval training (HIIT), they are designed to enhance cardiovascular endurance while boosting coordination and agility.

Here's how to perform jumping jacks with maximum effectiveness:

1. **Starting Position:**
   Stand tall with your feet together and arms relaxed at your sides. Embrace your energy and prepare for action!

2. **The Jump:**
   Propel yourself upwards! As you jump, swiftly spread your legs shoulder-width apart while simultaneously raising your

arms overhead until your palms almost touch. Imagine reaching for the sky as you elevate your heart rate.

3. **Return:**
Jump again, bringing your legs back together and lowering your arms to your sides in a smooth, controlled motion. Feel the flow of energy as you transition between movements.

4. **Flow:**
Keep repeating these movements rhythmically and continuously. The alternating action of spreading and closing your legs while raising and lowering your arms not only provides an excellent full-body workout but also keeps your heart pumping!

Pro Tips for Perfecting Your Jumping Jacks:

- Land softly on the balls of your feet to minimize impact on your knees, promoting a safer and more effective workout.

- Engage your core to maintain stability and ensure your back stays straight throughout each repetition. This will help you build strength and improve form.

- Incorporate jumping jacks into your fitness routine regularly to fortify your cardiovascular system and enhance overall athletic performance.

Get ready to jump into a healthier, stronger you! Embrace this simple yet powerful exercise, feel the burn, and celebrate every successful repetition along the way!

UNLOCK YOUR EXPLOSIVE POWER!

Jump squats, a dynamic plyometric exercise, are your ticket to skyrocketing explosive power and speed. By merging the classic squat with an exhilarating jump, this exercise not only targets your leg and glute muscles but also ramps up your cardiovascular endurance. When executed with precision, jump squats can significantly enhance your jumping ability. However, mastering the technique is essential to minimize injury risk and maximize your gains!

How to Nail Jump Squats:

1. **Starting Position:**
   Set yourself up for success! Stand tall with your feet shoulder-width apart and toes slightly turned outward. You can extend your arms to shoulder height, keep them at your sides, or cross them confidently over your chest.

2. **Lowering Phase:**
   Sink into the squat position by pushing your hips back and
   bending your knees until your thighs are parallel to the
   ground—or as low as your flexibility permits. Keep your
   weight anchored in your heels and ensure that your knees
   stay behind your toes for optimal safety.

3. **The Jump:**
   From the depths of your squat, propel yourself upward
   with explosiveness! Drive through your heels to initiate the
   jump, using the strength of your entire body. Let your arms
   swing down for momentum, then drive them up forcefully
   to help lift you higher.

4. **Landing:**
   Land gracefully on the balls of your feet, transitioning
   smoothly through the entire foot surface. Bend your knees
   to absorb the impact and prepare for the next squat—this
   will protect your joints and facilitate a fluid rhythm.

5. **Repetitions:**
   Choose a set number of repetitions or challenge yourself
   in timed intervals (e.g., 30 seconds) to elevate the intensity
   of your workout.

Common Mistakes to Avoid:

- Landing with a slack posture increases injury risk.

- Jumping too low or losing form can strain your joints.

- Leaning forward excessively may lead to back discomfort.

Jump squats are an incredibly effective way to amplify the
intensity of your workouts and enhance overall muscle
functionality. By adhering to proper technique and form, you
can harness this explosive exercise to boost both your

explosiveness and overall body fitness. Embrace the journey and watch yourself soar!

STRENGTHEN YOUR CORE LIKE NEVER BEFORE!

Lying leg raises, often referred to as leg lifts, are a powerhouse exercise for targeting the lower abdominal region while also engaging your hip flexors and enhancing core stability. When performed with precision, this exercise not only builds a robust core but also sets the foundation for better overall fitness.

Getting Started with Lying Leg Raises: To kick off your workout, find a comfortable, firm surface and lie flat on your back. Extend your legs fully, letting your arms rest naturally at your sides. You can choose to place your palms either down on the floor or tucked gently beneath your glutes for extra lower back support.

Mastering the Correct Form:

1. **Engage Your Core:**
   Tighten your abdomen and press your lower back firmly into the floor to stabilize your lumbar spine.

2. **Lift with Purpose:**
   Inhale deeply and simultaneously lift both legs straight off the floor, ensuring that you keep your pelvis stable and avoid any arching in your lower back.

3. **Achieve the Right Angle:**
   Raise your legs until they create a 90-degree angle with the floor, or as high as possible without straining your back muscles. Remember, slow and controlled movements are key!

4. **Pause in Power:**
   Hold this position momentarily to maintain tension in your core.

5. **Lower with Control:**
   Exhale as you gently lower your legs back down without letting them touch the floor. This maintains continuous engagement of your abdominal muscles and prevents any sagging of the back.

6. **Repeat:**
   Complete the desired number of sets and repetitions while focusing on form.

Common Pitfalls to Avoid: Be cautious not to lower your legs too far; doing so may cause your lower back to lift off the ground, leading to discomfort or potential pain.

Advanced Variations to Challenge Yourself:

- Bent Leg Raises

- Hanging Leg Raises

- Leg Raises with a Ball or Weight Between Your Feet

- Scissor Kicks

Lying leg raises are not just an exercise but a commitment to strengthening your lower abdominal muscles. Remember, maintaining concentration on technique and keeping core tension throughout each rep is essential for optimal results. Embrace the challenge, stay focused, and unlock a stronger core today!

Lunges, often celebrated as a dynamic lower-body exercise, are an excellent way to strengthen and sculpt your legs. This powerful movement primarily engages key muscle groups, including the quadriceps (the muscles at the front of your thighs), glutes, hamstrings (the muscles at the back of your thighs), and to some extent, your core for stabilization.

Mastering the Art of Lunges: A Step-by-Step Guide

1. **Starting Position:**
   Begin by standing tall with your feet hip-width apart. Keep your torso straight and your gaze forward.

2. **Executing a Lunge:**
   Step boldly forward with one leg. As you lower into the lunge, bend both knees—aim to bring your back knee close to the ground while ensuring your front knee forms a perfect 90-degree angle. Remember, your front knee should never extend beyond your toes for safety.

3. **Returning to Starting Position:**
   Powerfully push off with your front foot to return to the starting stance.

4. **Switching Sides:**
   Now, repeat the movement with your other leg, creating a balanced workout.

Pro Tips for Effective Lunges:

- Perform each lunge with controlled precision to reduce the risk of injury.

- Keep your upper body upright and avoid leaning forward.

- For an added challenge and extra core engagement, consider holding dumbbells or placing a barbell on your shoulders.

- Ensure smooth and fluid movements—avoid any jerky motions for better stability.

Lunges are incredibly versatile! You can modify them in various ways to target specific muscles or adjust their difficulty. Consider trying reverse lunges, side lunges, or walking lunges to diversify your routine. These exercises are fantastic additions to any full-body or leg-focused workout, empowering you on your journey to strength and resilience!

MOUNTAIN CLIMBERS

Mountain climbers are an exceptional full-body workout that effectively targets your cardiovascular system and core muscles. This dynamic exercise combines the stabilizing benefits of a plank with the invigorating motion of running, making it perfect for enhancing endurance and elevating your heart rate.

Why Mountain Climbers Benefit You

With every rep, you not only strengthen your core, but you also boost your cardiovascular fitness—making it a powerful tool for anyone looking to push their limits.

How to Execute Mountain Climbers with Precision

1. **Starting Position:**
   Begin in a plank position, placing your hands firmly on the ground about shoulder-width apart. Your arms should be

extended, and your body should form a straight line from your heels to your head.

2. **Performing the Movement:**
   Engage your core by pulling your right knee toward your chest while keeping your hips level. Maintain a strong, stable position throughout the exercise.

3. **Return to Starting Position:**
   Quickly return to the plank by straightening your right leg while simultaneously bringing your left knee toward your chest.

4. **Alternating Reps:**
   Continue alternating legs rapidly, mimicking the motion of running in place. Visualize yourself conquering a steep mountain—hence the name "Mountain Climbers."

Pro Tips for Maximum Effectiveness:

- **Maintain Proper Posture:**
  Keep your back straight and avoid raising or lowering your hips. Your body should remain in a straight line from head to heels.

- **Engage Your Core:**
  Keeping your abs tight throughout the movement is crucial for strengthening and protecting your core.

- **Adjust Your Pace:**
  Tailor the speed of your workout to meet your fitness goals. A faster pace will elevate your heart rate for an intense cardio burn, while a slower tempo will better focus on core strength development.

- **Increase the Challenge:**
  For an added difficulty level, try using sliding pads or TRX slings for a new twist on this classic exercise.

Mountain climbers are incredibly versatile, making them ideal for high-intensity interval training (HIIT) or circuit workouts. Incorporate them into your routine to enhance both aerobic and anaerobic conditioning, setting you on the path to achieving peak physical performance!

SLOW-MOTION MOUNTAIN CLIMBERS

Elevate Your Workout Experience

While traditional fast-paced mountain climbers prioritize endurance and cardiovascular fitness, the slow-motion variation takes your training to the next level by honing in on muscle control, balance, and stability.

- **Pace:**
  Embrace a slow and controlled movement, allowing for deeper engagement of your muscles.

- **Goal:**
  The primary aim is to enhance muscle activation, control, and stability, providing you with a strong foundation for all your fitness endeavors.

- **Focus:**
  This exercise emphasizes core strength and stability while significantly improving your balance.

- **Movement:**
  Deliberately draw one knee to your chest, ensuring that you control every phase of the movement. This precision is key to maximizing your results.

- **Intensity:**
  While the cardiovascular intensity may be lower, the

muscle demand is higher due to the extended time under tension, making each rep count.

- **Balance:**
  Experience an increased emphasis on coordination and balance skills that will serve you well in all activities.

Transform your workout routine with slow-motion mountain climbers and discover the power of mindfulness in movement. Your body and mind will thank you!

ELEVATE YOUR CORE STRENGTH

Unlock the power of your core with **Oblique V-Ups**, the ultimate exercise specifically designed to target and strengthen your obliques. Not only do these challenging moves elevate your oblique muscle activation, but they also enhance core stability and fortify the deeper muscles within your core. To achieve optimal results and minimize the risk of injury, mastering proper form is essential.

Starting Position:
Begin by lying comfortably on one side of your body, ensuring that your legs are extended and aligned with your torso, while keeping your head in a neutral position. For added stability, place your bottom hand flat on the floor in front of you. Your top hand can either rest gently behind your head or rest on your side oblique for extra balance.

How to Perform Oblique V-Ups:

1. **Engage Your Core**:
   Activate your obliques by drawing your belly button toward your spine, preparing for the lift.

2. **Lift with Intent**:
   In one smooth, controlled motion, simultaneously raise both your upper body and legs using the strength of your obliques as the driving force.

3. **Form the "V"**:
   Aim to lift your legs high enough that your body forms a striking "V" shape, reaching for the toes of your elevated legs with your hand.

4. **Pause at Peak Tension**:
   After reaching maximum tension in your obliques, hold this powerful position for a moment to accentuate the engagement.

5. **Lower with Control**:
   Gently return to the starting position without resting on the floor, maintaining control throughout the descent.

Technical Tips:

- **Control is Key**:
  Resist the temptation to use momentum; rely on controlled contraction of your obliques for movement.

- **Alignment Matters**:
  Keep your head and neck in line with your spine to avoid unnecessary strain.

- **Prioritize Form Over Extremes**:
  Strive for that perfect "V" shape, but listen to your body—maintaining good form is always more important than achieving perfection.

Common Missteps:

- **Hip Sagging**:
  A strong core is essential to prevent sagging. Focus on engaging your core muscles fully.

- **Uncontrolled Movements**:
  Embrace slow, deliberate movements for safety and effectiveness.

- **Avoid Head Strain**:
  The top hand should not pull or push on the head; instead, concentrate on contracting those vital obliques.

Integrate **Oblique V-Ups** into your core workout and unleash their potential for strengthening and defining your obliques. By doing so, you will not only enhance muscle balance and symmetry but also elevate your overall core performance. Embrace this challenge and empower yourself to achieve new heights!

PUSH-UPS

Push-ups are one of the most effective and time-tested exercises for building upper body strength and muscle. Not only do they target the pectorals, triceps, and shoulders, but they also engage your core, making them a fantastic full-body workout.

To maximize your push-up performance and ensure you're getting the most out of this exercise, here are some key components to keep in mind:

1. **Hand and Arm Position:**
   Begin by placing your hands flat on the floor, shoulder-width apart. Your fingers should point forward or be slightly angled outward to reduce strain on your wrists. Start with your arms fully extended, but keep your elbows slightly bent to protect your joints.

2. **Posture:**
   Maintain a straight line from your heels to your head throughout the movement. Avoid letting your hips sag too low or rise too high, as both can lead to improper form and strain. Engage your abdominal and gluteal muscles to stabilize your core, protecting your lower back and enhancing overall body control.

3. **Downward Movement:**
   As you lower yourself, keep your elbows angled slightly

back and close to your body rather than flaring out. Aim to lower yourself until your chest or chin nearly touches the ground.

4. **Upward Movement:**
   Push yourself back up with controlled power until your arms are almost fully extended—again, take care not to lock your elbows completely. Ensure that your body remains in a straight line during this phase as well.

5. **Variations:**
   To target different muscle groups or ramp up the intensity, experiment with variations. Close-grip push-ups focus on the triceps, while elevated push-ups can increase difficulty. You might even try explosive push-ups for an added challenge that requires lifting your hands off the floor.

By mastering these elements and incorporating variations, you'll not only strengthen your upper body but also cultivate the mental resilience needed to push past physical limits. Embrace the challenge and empower yourself on this journey!

ELEVATE YOUR CORE STRENGTH AND STABILITY

L ooking to strengthen your core while enhancing your shoulder stability and balance? Plank shoulder taps are an outstanding exercise that combines the foundational benefits of the plank with a dynamic movement, elevating both your coordination and body awareness.

What You'll Gain: Engaging in plank shoulder taps primarily targets your core, shoulders, and arms, promoting improved stability and balance. This exercise not only strengthens your body but also cultivates greater body awareness and coordination skills.

Get Started: The Perfect Plank Position

1. **Starting Position:**
   Begin in a solid plank position with your hands directly beneath your shoulders and your feet hip-width apart. Ensure that your body forms a straight line from head to toe, with your core engaged.

2. **Core Stabilization:**
   Activate those abdominal muscles to maintain a stable spine and prevent any sagging in your lower back. Don't forget to engage your glutes to uphold a straight posture.

3. **The Tapping Motion:**
   Slowly lift your right hand off the ground, gently tapping your left shoulder while maintaining as much stability as possible in the rest of your body. Lower your right hand back down with control before switching to the left hand and tapping the right shoulder.

4. **Alternating Sides:**
   Continue to alternate between hands without twisting or rocking your hips—the key to this movement is core stability!

Common Mistakes and How to Fix Them:

- **Hips Twisting:**
  Keep those hips steady for maximum stability; widening your foot stance can enhance hip stabilization.

- **Back Sagging:**
  Ensure your core is actively engaged to avoid sagging in the lower back.

- **Lack of Core Tension:**
  Maintain tight abs and glutes throughout for spine stabilization.

- **Fast, Uncontrolled Movements:**
  Emphasize slow, controlled motions to fully engage the muscles and reduce injury risk.

Exciting Variations of Plank Shoulder Taps:

- **Elevated Plank Shoulder Taps:**
  Use an elevated surface like a bench to lessen wrist strain; perfect for beginners!

- **Weighted Plank Shoulder Taps:**
  Incorporate light dumbbells in your hands for an added challenge to arm muscles.

- **Plank Shoulder Taps with Alternating Leg Raises:**
  Raise the opposite leg while tapping the shoulder; this heightens difficulty and promotes balance.

- **Plank Shoulder Taps on an Unstable Surface:**
  Challenge yourself by using a Bosu ball or balance pads to train stability.

- **Dynamic Plank Shoulder Taps:**
  Combine with other dynamic exercises like plank reaches or push-ups for an even more stimulating workout!

Alternative Exercises:

- **Plank-to-Knee Touches:**
  Gently touch the opposite knee with one hand while maintaining plank form; great for beginners!

- **Plank with Arm Lift:**
  Lift one arm forward without making contact with the opposite shoulder to focus more on shoulder strength.

- **Side Plank with Hip Dips:**
  Transition into a side plank position, lowering and rising your hip for stronger obliques and improved core stability.

- **Bird-Dog:**
  On all fours, extend one arm forward while reaching back with the opposite leg; enhances balance and core strength.

Embrace the Power of Plank Shoulder Taps! Incorporate plank shoulder taps into your routine for effective gains in core stability, balance, and coordination. By mastering the fundamentals and exploring various modifications, you can tailor this exercise to fit any fitness level while keeping your workouts fresh and engaging. Embrace these techniques today and experience optimal results in your training journey!

MASTER THE PLANK: UNLOCK YOUR CORE STRENGTH

The plank, also known as the forearm plank, is a powerhouse isometric exercise designed to fortify your core muscles. This deceptively simple yet incredibly challenging movement can seamlessly fit into any fitness routine, making it a must-try for anyone looking to enhance their strength and stability. By engaging the abs, lower back, and shoulders, the plank not only boosts your posture but also lays the groundwork for functional strength in daily activities and athletic endeavors. To truly harness these benefits, it's crucial to master the plank technique.

Here's how to perform a plank correctly:

1. **Starting Position:**
   Start on all fours, placing your elbows directly under your

shoulders. Your forearms should rest flat on the floor, and you can choose to clench your fists, press your hands flat, or clasp them together—pick the variation that feels best for you.

2. **Body Alignment:**
Slide your legs back and lift your hips until your body forms a straight line from shoulders to heels. Steer clear of sagging your lower back or lifting your butt too high; both mistakes can undermine the effectiveness of the exercise and lead to injury.

3. **Core Activation:**
Engage your entire core by bracing your abdominal muscles as if you're bracing for a punch. Keep your glutes and hamstrings tight as well. This core tension stabilizes your pelvis and protects your lower back.

4. **Gaze Direction and Neck Position:**
Maintain a neutral neck position by gazing downwards, allowing your spine to extend naturally. Avoid tilting or lowering your head to prevent unnecessary neck strain.

5. **Duration:**
Aim to hold the position for a set time—typically 20 seconds to several minutes—depending on your fitness level. Remember, maintaining proper form takes precedence over prolonging the hold; prioritize technique over duration.

Variations for Extra Challenge:

- **Knee Plank:**
Keep your knees on the floor for support.

- **Side Plank:**
Engage the obliques by balancing on one arm.

- **Plank with Movement:**
  Incorporate walking movements with arms or legs for an added challenge.

- **Elevated Plank:**
  Increase difficulty by placing hands on an exercise ball.

Common Mistakes to Avoid:

- **Hips Too High or Low:**
  This decreases core engagement and can lead to back pain.

- **Swayback:**
  Tighten those abdominal muscles to prevent sagging.

- **Tense Neck:**
  Keep your neck relaxed and neutral without tilting up or down.

A well-executed plank creates strength and stability throughout the entire body. By incorporating this effective exercise into your fitness regimen regularly and gradually increasing hold times, you'll fortify your core, elevate your performance, and feel empowered in every workout. Get ready to plank it out!

RUSSIAN TWISTS

Russian twists are a dynamic and highly effective exercise for strengthening the abdominal muscles, particularly the obliques, while enhancing overall core stability. This versatile workout can be done with or without weights, making it an excellent addition to any core training routine or circuit workout.

How to Perform Russian Twists Correctly:

- **Starting Position:**
  Begin by sitting on the floor with your knees bent and feet flat on the ground. Lean your upper body back slightly to create a 45-degree angle between your thighs and torso. Ensure your back remains straight to maintain proper alignment.

- **Positioning Your Arms:**
  You can either clasp your hands together in front of you or hold a weight, such as a dumbbell or a medicine ball, for a more challenging variation that amplifies the benefits of this exercise.

- **The Twist:**
  Initiate the movement by gently rotating your upper body, along with your arms or the weight, from side to side without altering the position of your legs. Remember to

keep your back straight and engage your core throughout the motion.

- **Continuing the Exercise:**
  Repeat the twisting motions for your desired number of repetitions or for a set duration.

Tips for Mastering Russian Twists Effectively:

- Focus on engaging your core muscles rather than merely swinging your arms.

- For an added challenge, lift your feet off the floor while performing the twists to engage additional stabilizing muscles.

- Avoid excessive arching of your lower back to prevent discomfort and injury.

- Start at a slow pace, especially when incorporating weights, and gradually increase intensity to safely build strength.

- Maintain balance and proper form by keeping your gaze on your hands or weight as you twist, ensuring that your movements are controlled and focused.

Russian twists are not just beneficial for sculpting the abdominal area; they significantly enhance coordination and balance as well. By incorporating this exercise into your fitness routine, you're on track to unlocking greater physical stability and achieving your health goals. Embrace the challenge and let each twist empower you on your journey toward peak performance!

A POWERFUL EXERCISE FOR CORE STRENGTH AND STABILITY

The side plank is an incredibly effective bodyweight exercise designed to strengthen your core and oblique muscles. This dynamic movement also targets your lower back, hips, and shoulders, making it a comprehensive addition to your fitness routine. As a variation of the traditional plank, the side plank excels in enhancing balance and stability, empowering you to challenge your physical limits.

How to Execute the Side Plank:

1. **Start Position:**
   Begin by lying on your side with your legs straight, one foot directly on top of the other.

2. **Setup:**
Support your body with your extended arm, placing your palm firmly on the floor directly under your shoulder.

3. **Alignment:**
Ensure that your body forms a straight line from your feet to your head.

4. **Lift Off:**
Engage your core to raise your hips off the ground until your body is in a perfect alignment.

5. **Maintain Position:**
Keep your hips elevated, avoiding any forward or backward tilting.

6. **Brace Yourself:**
Tighten your abdomen while stabilizing your shoulder above the elbow (for forearm variation) or hand (for hand variation).

7. **Hand Placement:**
You can place one hand on your hip or extend it upwards for added balance.

8. **Hold Steady:**
Maintain this position for a duration that suits your fitness level and training plan.

9. **Switch Sides:**
Don't forget to repeat the exercise on the other side!

Common Mistakes and Corrections:

- **Sinking Hips:**
Ensure you lift your hips properly so that your body maintains a straight line.

- **Losing Tension:**
  Keep your core engaged throughout the exercise to maximize effectiveness.

- **Incorrect Head Position:**
  Look straight ahead to keep your neck aligned with your spine.

- **Shoulder Stability:**
  Avoid hunching or dropping the shoulder; it should be positioned directly above the elbow or hand.

Variations to Challenge Yourself:

- **Top Leg Raise:**
  Elevate the top leg for an added challenge to your balance and strength.

- **Torso Rotation:**
  Incorporate a torso twist for an advanced level of engagement.

- **Hip Lifts:**
  Add controlled hip lifts to intensify the workout.

Embrace the side plank as not just an exercise, but a step toward fortified core muscles and enhanced stability! With dedication and practice, you'll build resilience not only in strength but also in confidence, preparing you to conquer greater physical challenges ahead. Let's push those boundaries together!

UNLEASH YOUR INNER ATHLETE

Sprinting in place is a dynamic, high-intensity exercise designed to supercharge your cardiovascular fitness, enhance leg strength, and build core stability—particularly targeting those all-important abdominal muscles. What's great about this exercise is its versatility; you can do it virtually anywhere, making it perfect for home workouts or as an exciting addition to your six-pack training routine.

Why Sprint in Place? This powerful exercise focuses on boosting endurance, engaging your leg and calf muscles, and activating your core. It's time to push your limits and elevate your fitness game!

1. Starting Position:

    - Stand tall with your feet hip-width apart.

    - Let your arms hang loosely at your sides, ready to spring into action.

2. The Sprinting Motion:

    - Drive your knees up towards your chest as high as possible, alternating swiftly between legs. Imagine the speed of a true sprint!

- Minimize ground contact with your feet for a light, bouncy motion.

- Swing your arms rhythmically in tandem with your legs to simulate an authentic running experience.

3. Posture Matters:

- Keep your upper body upright and shoulders relaxed.

- Engage your abdominal muscles to promote stability throughout the sprint.

Common Mistakes & How to Fix Them:

- **Knees Too Low:**
Aim to raise those knees higher for optimal core and leg activation!

- **Uncoordinated Arm Movements:**
Ensure your arms are moving fluidly with your legs—this balance is key!

- **Hunched Back:**
Maintain an erect posture; a straight back is essential for effective sprinting.

Exciting Variations of Sprinting in Place:

- **High-Knee Sprints:**
Amp up the intensity by driving those knees even higher while quickening your pace. This targets the abs and hip flexors!

- **Butt Kicks:**
Instead of driving knees forward, pull heels toward your glutes. This variation challenges the hamstrings and glutes more intensely.

- **Arm Movement Sprint:**
Incorporate powerful arm movements by raising them overhead with each knee lift. This not only boosts intensity but also engages shoulder muscles.

- **Lateral Sprinting:**
Add a lateral twist by lifting knees out to the side. This variation enhances lateral mobility and balance.

- **Dumbbell Sprinting:**
Hold light dumbbells as you sprint in place, adding resistance that intensifies the workout for your arms and shoulders.

Alternative Exercises:

If you want to mix things up or need modifications, consider these alternatives:

- **Mountain Climbers:**
Start in a plank position and rapidly draw knees toward your chest. This fiery exercise targets the core while ramping up cardiovascular fitness.

- **High Knees:**
Run in place while bringing knees as high as possible—don't forget to swing those arms! This boosts both endurance and coordination.

- **Jump Squats:**
Begin with a squat and explode upward into a jump. Land softly and descend into another squat. This move strengthens legs and enhances explosive power!

Sprinting in place is an incredible weapon for improving endurance, leg strength, and core stability. By mastering the fundamentals and exploring various adaptations, you can tailor this exercise to fit your fitness level while keeping workouts fresh and challenging. So, unleash the power within you! Regularly incorporate sprinting in place into your training routine for spectacular results—let's chase greatness together!

IMITATION JUMP ROPE

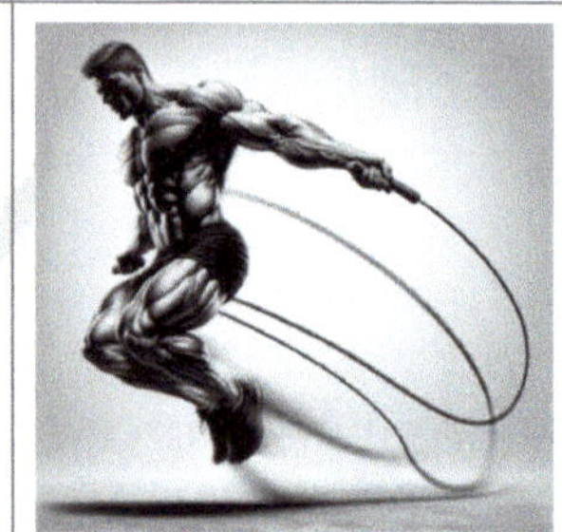

ELEVATE YOUR CARDIO AND AGILITY WORKOUTS!

The imitation jump rope is an exhilarating high-intensity cardio workout that not only boosts your endurance but also enhances your coordination and agility. If you don't have a jump rope on hand, fear not! Imitation jump rope provides similar benefits to traditional jumping without the need for any equipment. In this article, you'll discover how to perform imitation jump rope correctly, along with exciting variations to spice up your routine.

UNLEASH YOUR POTENTIAL

Imitation jump rope maximizes cardiovascular fitness while strengthening your leg muscles, calves, and overall coordination. Best of all, you can do it anywhere! It's perfect as a warm-up or as part of a dynamic interval workout.

Getting Started:

1. Starting Position:

   - Stand tall with your feet hip-width apart.

   - Slightly bend your arms and position your hands at hip height, as if holding an imaginary rope.

2. Jumping Technique:

   - **Jumping:** Lightly spring off the ground with both feet, landing softly on the balls of your feet.

   - **Arm Movement:** Rotate your forearms and wrists as though you're swinging a rope. This action enhances coordination and gives an authentic feel to your jumping.

3. Posture Matters:

   - Keep your upper body upright and shoulders relaxed.

   - Engage your core muscles to maintain stability throughout the exercise.

Common Mistakes & How to Fix Them:

- **Jumping Too High:**
  Keep jumps light and controlled for maximum efficiency while protecting your joints.

- **Incorrect Arm Technique:**
  Ensure your arms and wrists rotate fluidly to effectively mimic the swing of a real rope.

- **Unstable Posture:**
  Maintain a stable upper body, evenly distributing weight between both legs.

Exciting Variations to Try:

1. High-Knee Imitation Jump Rope:
   As you jump, lift your knees toward your hips alternately. This variation elevates the intensity and engages your thigh and hip muscles.

2. One-Legged Imitation Jump Rope:
   Jump on one leg while keeping the other slightly raised. Switch legs after a designated number of jumps. This version improves balance and targets specific leg muscles.

3. Lateral Imitation Jump Rope:
   Leap sideways to the left and right as if swinging an imaginary rope. This trains lateral leg muscles and boosts coordination.

4. Double-Under Imitation Jump Rope:
   Simulate two quick turns of the rope for each jump by speeding up your wrist rotation. This variation intensifies the workout and enhances explosive strength.

5. Combination of Imitation Jump Rope & Jumping Jacks:
   Integrate jumping jacks by spreading and bringing back together your legs with each jump. This combo increases cardiovascular intensity while adding variety to lower body movements.

Alternatives to Enhance Your Workout:

If imitation jump rope isn't quite what you're looking for, or if you're seeking similarly effective exercises, consider these fantastic alternatives:

1. **Knee Lift Run:**
   Jog in place while alternating knee lifts to hip height and swinging your arms. This move enhances cardio fitness and strengthens leg muscles.

2. **Jumping Jacks:**
   Jump while moving your legs apart and arms overhead, then return to the starting position. Jumping jacks target cardiovascular fitness and improve coordination.

3. **Box Jumps:**
   Leap onto an elevated platform (like a box or bench) with both feet, then step back down. This exercise boosts explosive power and develops leg strength.

The imitation jump rope is a powerful and versatile exercise for enhancing cardiovascular health and coordination. By mastering the basics and experimenting with various modifications, you can tailor this routine to suit your fitness level—creating an engaging and challenging workout every time! Embrace these variations and alternatives, incorporating imitation jump rope into your training regimen for optimal results! Get ready to push your limits and achieve new heights!

STRENGTHEN YOUR CORE AND IMPROVE POSTURE

The Superman Hold is a powerhouse bodyweight exercise that effectively isolates and strengthens the stabilizing muscles of your lower back, glutes, and shoulders. This dynamic movement also engages the muscles along your spine and hip extensors, contributing to better posture and overall stability.

How to Perform the Superman Hold:

1. **Starting Position:**
   Begin by lying flat on your stomach on a comfortable surface. Extend your arms straight out in front of you, keeping your legs straight and together. Maintain a neutral position by gazing downward to protect your neck.

2. **Lifting Your Body:**
   With control, lift your upper body and legs off the floor simultaneously. Your abdomen and pelvis should remain grounded while your arms stay fully extended. Focus on engaging your core throughout this movement.

3. **Holding the Position:**
   Keep this elevated position for 10 to 30 seconds, depending on your current strength level. Remember to breathe evenly—holding your breath will only increase tension!

4. **Returning to Start Position:**
   Gently lower your upper body and legs back to the starting position. Take a moment to reset before attempting again.

Pro Tips for Success:

- **Neck Alignment:**
  Keep your neck neutral to minimize strain.

- **Progress Gradually:**
  Start with shorter intervals and work your way up as your strength increases.

- **Stay Smooth:**
  Avoid any jerky or rapid movements to prevent discomfort or injury.

Embrace the challenge of the Superman Hold as a vital step towards building mental resilience and physical strength. Remember, every second counts—celebrate each small victory along the way!

SPIDERMAN PUSH-UPS

Spiderman push-ups are an exciting twist on the classic push-up, designed to amp up your workout and engage additional muscle groups. This variation incorporates a dynamic movement where you'll bring your knee toward the same-side elbow during the downward phase, effectively targeting your core, particularly those oblique abdominal muscles.

Here's how to perform Spiderman push-ups correctly:

- **Starting Position:**
  Begin in a standard push-up position with your arms fully extended and hands placed flat on the floor, shoulder-width apart. Your feet should also be shoulder-width apart, and your body should form a straight line from your head to your heels.

- **Downward Movement:**
  Lower your body by bending your elbows, just like you would in a traditional push-up.

- **Knee Movement:**
  As you lower yourself, draw your knee sideways towards your same-side elbow. Your knee should glide outward along the side of your body.

- **Upward Movement:**
  Push yourself back up to the starting position while simultaneously extending your leg back out.

- **Switching Sides:**
  Repeat the movement on the opposite side, pulling the other knee toward its corresponding elbow during the next downward phase.

Tips for Effective Spiderman Push-Ups:

- Engage your core muscles tightly throughout the exercise to maintain stability.

- Keep your hips from sagging and ensure your neck stays in a neutral position.

- Move slowly and with control to maximize effectiveness.

- If you're finding this exercise challenging, consider practicing with your knees on the ground or using an elevated surface to gradually build strength until you're ready for full intensity.

Spiderman push-ups aren't just a challenge; they combine strength and coordination, taking your push-up routine to the next level. Elevate your workouts by incorporating this vibrant exercise, and feel the benefits of engaging multiple muscle groups while honing both physical and mental resilience!

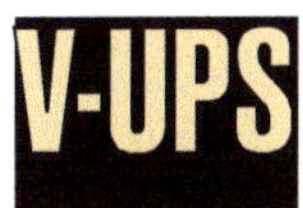

V-ups, often referred to as jackknife sit-ups, are a powerful and dynamic abdominal exercise that targets both your upper and lower core muscles while enhancing overall core stability. This exercise is highly sought after for its ability to engage multiple muscle groups effectively, leading to a stronger, more defined core. In this article, we will dive into the correct technique for performing V-ups and provide guidance on how to safely and effectively integrate them into your workout routine.

Step-by-Step Instructions for V-Ups

1. **Find Your Position:**
   Begin by lying flat on an exercise mat with your back aligned straight. Extend your arms overhead, keeping your legs straight and together.

2. **Activate Your Core:**
   Engage your abdominal muscles by gently pulling your abdominal wall inward. This will help stabilize your torso and protect your spine throughout the movement.

3. **Initiate the Movement:**
   Lift both your legs and upper body simultaneously, hinging at your hips and spine. Reach your hands toward your toes or at least toward your ankles.

4. **Form the "V":**
   At the peak of the movement, aim to create a "V" shape with your body, ensuring that only your buttocks remain in contact with the mat while your back is lifted off the ground. Maintain a forward gaze, keeping your neck aligned in a natural extension of your spine.

5. **Control Your Descent:**
   Slowly lower your upper body and legs back to the mat in
   a controlled manner, ensuring you don't lose contact with
   the floor.

6. **Repeat:**
   Complete the desired number of repetitions. Beginners
   may find 8-10 repetitions suitable, while seasoned athletes
   might aim for 12-20 or more per set.

Tips for Correct Execution

- **Control Your Movements:**
  Avoid any jerky motions; executing the exercise slowly and
  intentionally increases muscle activation and mitigates
  injury risk.

- **Prioritize Form Over Quantity:**
  Maintaining correct form is crucial—focus on technique
  rather than simply counting repetitions.

- **Gradually Increase Range of Motion:**
  Beginners may benefit from starting with a smaller range of
  motion and progressively increasing it as strength
  improves.

Common Mistakes to Avoid

- **Swinging Your Arms:**
  Ensure that you don't swing your arms; the power should
  arise from your core.

- **Dropping Too Low:**
  Steer clear of letting your legs and arms drop excessively
  at the end of the movement; maintain tension by avoiding
  contact with the ground.

- **Neglecting Your Lower Back:**
  Protecting your lower back is essential; avoid letting it sag
  to prevent discomfort or injury.

V-ups are not just an effective exercise; they can serve as a
pivotal component of any core workout, full-body routine, or
targeted ab session. By mastering the proper technique, you
can cultivate stronger abdominal muscles that enhance
control and balance throughout your entire body. Embrace
this challenge—your journey towards a resilient core starts
here!

WALL SIT

UNLOCK YOUR LEG STRENGTH

The wall sit, commonly referred to as a wall squat, is a
powerful static exercise designed to fortify your lower body,
particularly the quadriceps, glutes, and core. This isometric
hold has garnered popularity among athletes for its ability to

build both endurance and strength in the legs. Often utilized as a benchmark for muscular endurance, the wall sit challenges you to push past your limits while reinforcing correct form to help you achieve your fitness goals and protect your joints.

How to Perfect Your Wall Sit:

1. **Choose the Right Wall:**
   Look for a flat, stable wall that will provide the support you need during your exercise journey.

2. **Assume Your Starting Position:**
   Stand facing away from the wall, feet shoulder-width apart and approximately 2 feet from it. Lean back against the wall and gradually slide down until your knees form about a 90-degree angle.

3. **Maintain Correct Posture:**
   Ensure your thighs are parallel to the floor and that your knees are aligned directly over your ankles for optimal stability. Press your lower back against the wall to keep your spine straight, with your shoulders and head also supported against the surface.

4. **Hold the Position:**
   Rest your hands in your lap or position them in front of your chest to avoid relying on your arms for balance. Aim to hold this powerful position for a set amount of time based on your fitness level.

5. **Exit Gracefully:**
   To conclude the exercise, gently push yourself up the wall back to a standing position. Avoid abrupt movements when coming out of the wall sit to prevent unnecessary strain on your knees.

Tips for an Effective Wall Sit:

- Ensure your feet are firmly planted and do not slip.

- Engage your core by contracting your abdominal muscles to enhance stability.

- Keep those legs steady—avoid bending or rocking your knees during the hold for optimal tension.

Common Pitfalls to Avoid:

- **Incorrect Knee Angle:**
  A knee angle greater or less than 90 degrees can lead to unnecessary strain and diminish exercise effectiveness.

- **Relying on Your Hands:**
  Placing hands on your knees or thighs can relieve pressure from your legs and reduce the exercise's intensity.

- **Movement Away from the Wall:**
  Pushing your head and shoulders away from the wall can strain your neck and upper back muscles.

The wall sit is a versatile exercise that requires minimal space while effectively enhancing leg strength and endurance. By consistently incorporating this challenge into your training routine, you can elevate muscular

SHARE YOUR EXPERIENCES WITH US AND BECOME PART OF THE MMW COMMUNITY!

ABOUT THE AUTHOR

Autor: Alain Biankeu, Mighty Mind Warrior

Unlock your potential with this extraordinary book that serves as a beacon of inspiration! The author, celebrated for his uplifting outlook on life, masterfully guides us to embrace each day with confidence and joy. He understands that success is no accident—guided by the mantra, "Nothing comes from nothing," he embodies unwavering determination and demonstrates how hard work and consistency can help you conquer your goals.

This transformative book is packed with valuable principles and practical strategies for physical training and fitness, tailored for everyone, regardless of where they start. It powerfully illustrates the endless possibilities for personal growth and encourages you to commit to your journey of self-improvement. With a refreshing down-to-earth approach, the author's appreciation for life's small pleasures makes his insights not only relatable but deeply motivating.

Through relentless ambition and an eagerness to tackle new challenges, the author ignites a fire within you to strive for peak performance in training and elevate your fitness journey. Whether you're looking to enhance your health or cultivate a balanced lifestyle, this book is an essential companion on your path to becoming your best self.

Embrace the opportunity to discover how a positive mindset, dedicated effort, and an unstoppable drive can help you unlock your full physical potential. Allow this book to inspire you and reignite the joy in your training and pursuit of a fit lifestyle!